First published in the United States, Great Britain, Canada,
Australia, and New Zealand in 1994 by The Jane Goodall Institute.
Reissued in 1998 by North-South Books,
an imprint of Nord-Süd Verlag AG, Gossau Zürich, Switzerland.

Goodall, Jane.
With love : ten heartwarming stories of chimpanzees in the wild /
by Jane Goodall : illustrated by Alan Marks.
Summary : A collection of stories based on the author's experiences with chimpanzees
in Gombe Stream National Park in Tanzania over a period of almost forty years.
1. Chimpanzees—Tanzania—Gombe Stream National Park—Juvenile literature.
[1. Chimpanzees—Habits and behavior.] I. Marks, Alan. II. Title.
QL737.P96G588   1998
599.885—dc21   97-49948

A CIP catalogue record for this book is available from The British Library.
ISBN 1-55858-911-2 (trade binding)
3 5 7 9 TB 10 8 6 4 2
ISBN 1-55858-912-0 (library binding)
3 5 7 9 LB 10 8 6 4 2
Printed in Belgium

For more information about our books, and the authors and artists
who create them, visit our web site: http://www.northsouth.com

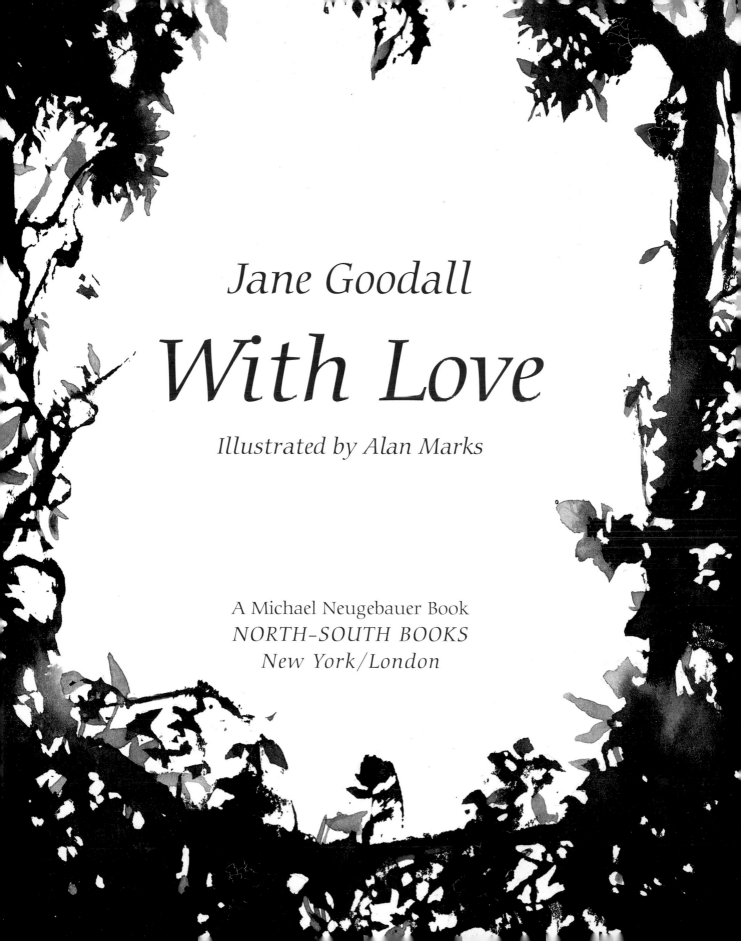

Jane Goodall

With Love

Illustrated by Alan Marks

A Michael Neugebauer Book
NORTH-SOUTH BOOKS
New York/London

INTRODUCTION

In 1960 almost nothing was known about the way chimpanzees live in the wild. That was when I went to Gombe National Park, in Tanzania, to see what I could find out. Every morning I climbed up into the forested mountains before it was light, and stayed up there until dusk. The chimpanzees were terrified of the peculiar white ape who had suddenly appeared in their world, and for months I could watch them only at a distance, through binoculars. If I tried to get too close, they fled. Gradually, though, some of them began to lose their fear.

One evening when I got back to camp, Dominic, my Tanzanian cook, told me that a large male chimpanzee had arrived that morning to feast on the ripe fruits of an oilnut palm growing by my tent. When he left, he had snatched some bananas from my table.

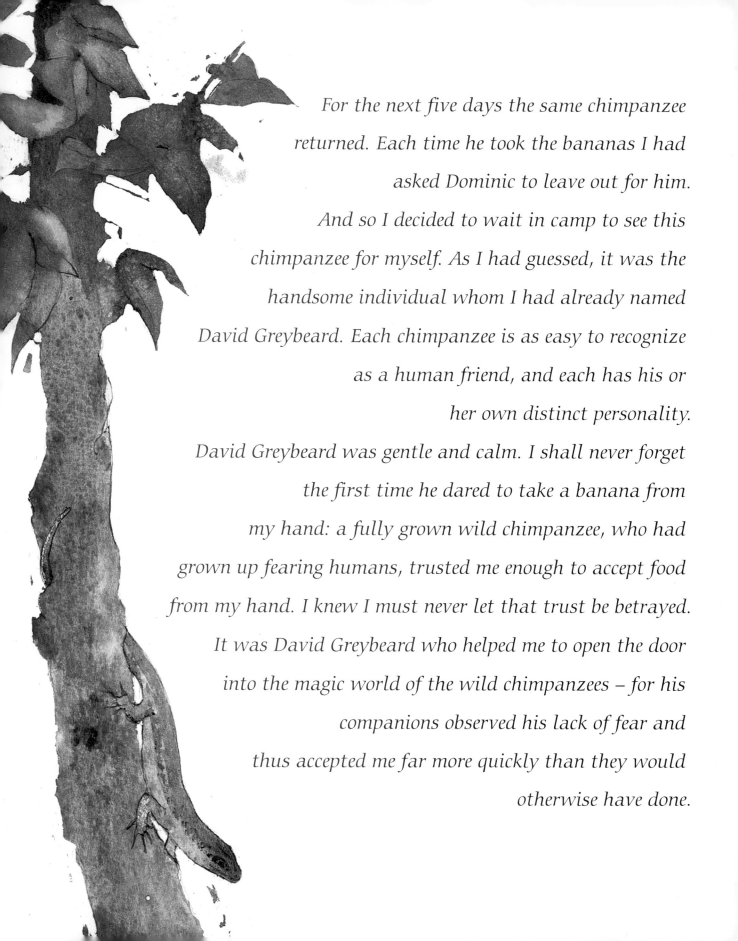

For the next five days the same chimpanzee returned. Each time he took the bananas I had asked Dominic to leave out for him. And so I decided to wait in camp to see this chimpanzee for myself. As I had guessed, it was the handsome individual whom I had already named David Greybeard. Each chimpanzee is as easy to recognize as a human friend, and each has his or her own distinct personality.

David Greybeard was gentle and calm. I shall never forget the first time he dared to take a banana from my hand: a fully grown wild chimpanzee, who had grown up fearing humans, trusted me enough to accept food from my hand. I knew I must never let that trust be betrayed. It was David Greybeard who helped me to open the door into the magic world of the wild chimpanzees – for his companions observed his lack of fear and thus accepted me far more quickly than they would otherwise have done.

David and the others have taught me much. Chimpanzees can, like humans, be very aggressive – even brutal – at times. But they can be so gentle, affectionate, and caring towards each other, too.

It is not only we humans who are capable of love, compassion, and altruism, and the stories recounted here – based on my experiences with chimpanzees over a period of almost forty years – demonstrate this capacity for love.

MEL AND SPINDLE

When Mel was just over three years old, his mother died during an epidemic of pneumonia that claimed the lives of seven other chimpanzees as well. In the wild, orphans are typically adopted and cared for by their elder sisters or brothers – but Mel was alone in the world. And anyway, like all three-year-olds, he was still drinking a good deal of milk – we all thought he would die. It wasn't even as though he was a robust infant. He was sickly and looked frail.

For the first couple of weeks Mel was a pathetic figure. He followed different chimpanzees, begging food from them, occasionally riding on their backs. They were, for the most part, tolerant of him – but he had no special friend, no individual on whom he could rely absolutely for comfort and protection.

And then the miracle happened. Mel was adopted by Spindle, a twelve-year-old adolescent male. Spindle was not closely related to Mel. Indeed, he had never even spent much time with the infant before. Yet now he waited for the orphan during travel, he allowed him to ride on his back or even, if it was raining or if Mel was frightened, to cling to his belly. Spindle always let the infant creep into his nest at night and, in response to Mel's begging gestures, often shared his food. And Spindle would run to defend or rescue his small charge if need arose.

Why did Spindle adopt Mel? We shall never know for sure. Was it,

perhaps, in some way connected with the fact that Spindle's mother, ancient Sprout, died at the same time as Mel's? Of course, a twelve-year-old male does not spend all that much time with his mother – he is off with the adult males, learning about hunting and protecting the territory, and about females. But even so, if his mother is still alive he often returns to her for a while if the going gets tough. In her familiar presence he finds reassurance and comfort. Is it possible that Sprout's death left an empty space in Spindle's heart, a space that was, to some extent, filled by his close contact with a small dependent infant?

Whatever the reason, Spindle saved Mel's life.

THE PIG HUNT

Chimpanzees enjoy eating fresh meat, and they occasionally hunt young bushpigs. This is sometimes dangerous, for wild pigs, as everyone knows, can be very fierce. One day a group of chimpanzees came across some adult pigs with young. The chimpanzees, bristling with excitement, began to hunt. They crashed about in the under-growth, making a lot of commotion, so that the pigs were confused and the hunters had more opportunity to seize a piglet. But even so, each time they tried, they were charged furiously by an adult pig.

Suddenly nine-year-old Freud began to scream in terror and pain. He was young to take part in a pig hunt and his lack of experience had landed him in trouble. He had managed to catch a piglet but he had not been quick enough to climb out of danger. One of the sows, desperately trying to protect her young, had charged Freud and bitten into his rump. There was the sound of tooth on bone.

The piglet escaped and ran off, unharmed.

Freud, screaming louder still, struggled to escape also, but the sow refused to let go. Suddenly a large chimpanzee burst from the under-growth, charging directly towards Freud and his captor. It was Gigi, large and childless, the Amazon of her community. The sow turned quickly to face this new challenge, and Freud, seizing his opportunity, painfully dragged himself up a tree.

Gigi herself only just escaped, leaping into some low branches with her foot only a few inches from the pig's powerful jaws.

Freud was badly hurt and bled heavily, and it was some weeks before he could walk without limping. Gigi had, without doubt, saved his life.

POM RESCUES HER INFANT BROTHER

One day, eight-year-old Pom was leading her family along a forest trail. Behind her tottered her three-year-old brother, Prof. Their mother, Passion, plodded some distance in the rear.

Suddenly Pom paused, staring at the ground ahead. There, coiled up in the thick undergrowth, was a big snake.

Pom uttered a small call of alarm and, with her hair bristling in fear, quickly climbed a nearby tree.

Prof, however, continued along the trail.

Perhaps he had not heard Pom's call, or had not under-stood what it meant. And Passion was not close enough to know what was happening. And so, with Pom watching from the branches above, Prof moved ever closer to the snake. Eventually, when he was but a few yards (metres) from it, Pom could bear it no longer. With her hair bristling even more, and a big grin of fear on her face, she leapt to the ground, gathered her little brother into her arms, and carried him back into the tree. They were safe, and gradually Pom's hair sleeked and the grin left her face.

By the time Passion arrived, the snake had glided away into the undergrowth.

PROF AND PAX

It was the rainy season, cold and wet. Not surprising that little Pax, just two years old, had a bad head cold.

His nose was stuffed up so that he breathed through his mouth, and he was listless, keeping close to his mother, Passion.

Presently his older brother, Prof, who was seven years old at this time, came over to enjoy a session of social grooming with Passion. Mostly it was she who groomed him, as is the way with mothers and sons. For a while Prof groomed young Pax, who was sitting, breathing noisily, beside them. Then he gave himself up to the soothing pleasure of his mother's gently grooming fingers.

Suddenly Pax was convulsed with a great sneeze. Prof, startled by the explosive sound, turned to look at his small brother. That sneeze had certainly cleared the stuffed-up nose – Pax was a disgusting sight at that moment. Better not to describe it! Prof stared for a moment and then reached out and picked a large handful of leaves. Very gently, very carefully, he wiped the snot from his brother's small face, peered briefly at the soiled leaves, then threw them away and again began grooming the infant. Passion, who had ignored the sneeze, continued to pay attention to her elder son.

Pax, his congestion at least temporarily relieved, and lulled by the rhythmic movements of grooming fingers, fell asleep.

MOTHER'S BOY

Sprout was a very ancient female indeed. At the time of this story she was at least forty years old, frail and all but toothless. Her twenty-five-year-old son, Satan, was, by contrast, in his prime – large, strong and magnificent.

One day, when many chimpanzees of the community were feasting on ripe figs and tension ran high, Satan persuaded his frequent ally Evered to join him in challenging the top-ranking male, Figan. But this plan backfired, for Evered, as soon as things warmed up, transferred his support to Figan. There was a furious skirmish high in the tree and Satan, outnumbered, began to scream loudly for help.

Old Sprout had been feeding peacefully in a nearby tree. But the

moment she heard her son's frenzied calling, she raced to his aid.
She leapt from branch to branch and, on arriving at the scene of the
battle, hurled herself into the fray. Evered, perhaps irritated by the
puny blows of this ancient and frail female, turned and began to hit
her – and Satan quickly seized the opportunity to pull away from
Figan and escape to the ground.

Now it was Sprout who screamed for help. It would be nice to relate
that Satan bravely returned to assist his mother. But no such thing
happened! Never mind – she was only cuffed a few times and
then she too escaped. Soon all was peaceful and the chimpanzees began to feed again. Satan fed close to his old mother.

FLO AND FLINT

Flo was a wonderful mother, patient, tolerant, affectionate, and playful. She gave her infants the opportunity to explore, yet she watched carefully, and at the slightest sign of real or imagined danger she would hasten to rescue them. In this way she successfully raised three offspring: Faben, Figan, and Fifi. Yet she failed both of her last youngsters.

When Flint was born, Flo already looked old. It was obvious that Faben had not been her first child – before conceiving him, she must have given birth at least twice to offspring who had either died or, if they were females, perhaps emigrated to nearby communities. For it is the females who sometimes disperse in chimpanzee society, thus preventing too much inbreeding. Be that as it may, at the time of Flint's birth Flo's teeth were already worn and her hair was thinning and brown with age. Despite this, Flo remained an aggressive and high-ranking female for the first couple of years of Flint's life. Things began to go wrong when Flint was four years old and Flo started the long process of weaning. The trouble was that Flint had become the chimpanzee equivalent of a "spoiled brat." Not only had he had the benefit of a dominant mother, always ready to protect and support him, but one or other of his elder brothers, or his sister, had usually been around, more than ready to help their young brother should he need them. Thus Flint became thoroughly used to

getting his own way. And when Flo tried to prevent him from suckling, or riding on her back, he resented it bitterly. He threw violent
tantrums. He even hit and bit his mother sometimes. Despite this,
Flo persisted in her efforts.

Things got even worse when, despite the fact that Flint was still
nursing, Flo became pregnant again. She needed all her failing
strength to nurture the life growing within her:
she had less and less energy to cope
with her obstreperous child.

Indeed, had her milk supply not dried up, Flint would have been suckling still when the next baby was born – a female whom we named Flame.

Flint became even more distressed – for now he had to share Flo's attention. He still tried to suckle, but despite his most violent tantrums, this was the one thing that Flo was firm about. However, she gave in when he insisted on riding on her back, and when he pushed into the night nest in the evening. And she acquiesced when he bothered her, endlessly, for social grooming. The burden on Flo grew even as Flame grew larger and Flint was still riding her back while Flame clung on below.

When Flame was six months old, she died. It happened when Flo herself was very, very sick, probably suffering from pneumonia. She lacked the strength to climb into the trees, and lay on the ground, often in the rain. When we found her, Flame had disappeared and we never knew what happened. Probably she died of the same disease, and bushpigs took away her little body.

Flo, to our amazement, recovered. And now, with Flame out of the way, Flint regained his former joie de vivre. But despite his loss of depression, he remained abnormally dependent on his old mother. He continued to sleep with her at night, and he stopped riding on her back only when she became so frail that her legs buckled under her when he climbed aboard. There were times when I felt like shaking

Flint because of the way he treated Flo. If she stopped to rest, he pestered her until she agreed to groom him. If he was ready to move on before his now ancient mother, he would sometimes push her from behind, whimpering like an infant. And because of him she had to construct, each night, a larger nest than would have been necessary for herself alone.

But then I realized that without Flint, Flo would have had a very lonely old age. For as she became ever more frail, she spent less and less time with the other chimps. She needed Flint for company. If they came to a fork in the trail and she went one way and he another, it was just as likely that she would give in and follow him as vice versa. Even daughter Fifi, her close companion until this time, abandoned her mother now. For Fifi had given birth. She had to travel further afield to find enough food for herself and her infant.

One day we found Flo's body lying at the edge of one of the fast-flowing streams. Flint was sitting on the bank, gazing down at her. Every so often he clambered down and peered at her closely. Sometimes he pulled at her dead hand, as though begging her to wake and groom him. Then, disconsolate, he climbed up and sat, huddled and miserable, looking down at his lifeless mother. That night he climbed slowly into a nearby tree and into a nest that, a few nights before, he had shared with Flo.

I climbed the steep hillside until I could see him where he lay. As darkness fell he was still staring, his eyes wide open, towards that sad place in the stream.

Flint gradually became more and more depressed. At first he spent a few days with his brother Figan. But suddenly he left the group and raced back to where he had left his mother.

She was gone by then – the bushpigs make short work of dead animals so we had taken her body for burial. Flint did not search for her. He resumed his huddled posture, sitting near the stream where she had died. Nothing seemed to bring him out of his depression. And by the time Fifi finally returned from a journey to the north, Flint had become sick. In his state of deep depression his immune system was probably so weakened that he had little resistance to infection.

Fifi did stay by him for a while. And he relaxed when she sat grooming him. But he lacked the strength, or the will, to follow when she moved on. And so, pausing many times to look back, she left him lying there. She never saw him again.

Flint died, three and a half weeks after losing his mother. I think the main cause of death was grief.

MADAM BEE AND HER DAUGHTER

Madam Bee was not as old as she looked. But for ten years she had
been afflicted by a paralyzed arm, the result of a polio epidemic that
had swept through Gombe. She had given birth to four offspring
but, probably because it had been so difficult for her to care for them
with only one good arm, the last two, born after the epidemic,
had died in infancy. Madam Bee's life had been a hard one.

Towards the end of her days, there was a very harsh dry season at Gombe. There was not much food and the chimpanzees had to walk long distances between one patch of fruit and the next. Madam Bee had just lost her last infant and these journeys exhausted her so that sometimes, when she finally reached her destination, she was too tired to climb.

This was hardly surprising, since she found it difficult to cope with tall trees at the best of times.

One day, after making such a long hot journey, Madam Bee lay stretched out on the ground and watched as her two daughters, adult Little Bee and adolescent Honey Bee, swung up to the high branches. With small calls of delight they began to feed on the ripe, juicy mabungo fruits. Only the old female's eyes indicated how much she longed to be up there too.

And then, after ten minutes, Little Bee started to collect fruits. They were large – tennis-ball sized – but she managed to carry three in her mouth with the stems between her teeth and two more in one hand. And then she climbed down and walked over to Madam Bee. She laid two of the fruits beside the old female and the two of them, mother and daughter, fed side by side, peaceful and content.

Little Bee was seen helping her mother on two other occasions.

GREMLIN AND GIMBLE

One day Gimble was following his mother, Melissa, through the long grass. Gremlin, his sister, brought up the rear. They were moving in single file, along one of the animal trails that wound its way across the top of an open ridge between two valleys. It was the end of the dry season, and the grass was as dry as straw.

Suddenly, as Melissa all but vanished where the trail led through an extra-tall patch of grass, Gremlin seized hold of her three-year-old brother and prevented him from following their mother. Gimble was bewildered and gave small cries of distress.

Gremlin struggled to gather him up, but he pulled away and tried to rush after Melissa, into the tall grass.

Quickly Gremlin pushed past her small brother and headed him off, shepherding him off the trail and insisting that he go around and not through that patch of long grass. Gimble's crying got louder, but soon the danger, whatever it might be, was safely passed and Gremlin allowed her brother to run after Melissa.

I went to look in the patch of tall grass. I moved cautiously, expecting to find a snake. At first I saw nothing – then suddenly I noticed that hundreds and hundreds of tiny ticks were clinging to the grass stems bordering the trail.

A whole brood must have just hatched.

Hastily I made the same detour that Gremlin had chosen for her brother. A while later Melissa stopped, and sitting in the shade, she began searching through her hair and picking off the many ticks that had dropped onto her as she passed by. They had already attached themselves, and probably their bites had begun to itch. Chimpanzees love to groom, as well as to be groomed, and Gremlin eagerly helped to detick her mother. But I didn't see her pick any off herself, and Gimble, thanks to his sister, was free as well. I still marvel at that chance observation. It was remarkable that Gremlin noticed those minute ticks from her position behind Gimble. That she would then avoid that place herself was not surprising. But how wonderful that, because of her concern, she had also saved her brother from the irritating bites.

AUNTIE GIGI

We have already met Gigi, when she rescued young Freud from the just vengeance of an angry bushpig. Large, destined never to bear a child, she behaves, in many ways, more like a male than a female. But she has always been fascinated by infants and, over the years, she has acted as "Auntie" to one youngster after another, playing with and grooming them. And, when the mothers permitted, carrying them during travel.

But however good those relationships were, the child's mother always came first. Until, when Gigi was about thirty-eight years old, came the epidemic that claimed eight chimpanzee lives, including the mothers of Mel and Spindle. That was the beginning of a new phase in Gigi's life.

I have already told how Spindle adopted Mel and saved his life. After a year, though, that relationship gradually weakened. And then Spindle disappeared, never to return. We presume he died. It was then that Mel began to follow Gigi. She did not carry him or share her nest, as Spindle had. But she waited for him before moving off. And if other youngsters threatened Mel, they had Gigi to answer to. During that same epidemic Little Bee also died. By that time she had given birth herself, and she left a child, Dar Bee, who was almost the same age as Mel. At first Dar Bee divided her time between three individuals: her juvenile brother, a young adult male, and an adolescent female. None of them nurtured her as Spindle nurtured Mel, not even her own brother. They all tolerated her presence, but she was not carried, and she slept in her own small nest at night. But, being a tough youngster, she survived.

And then Dar Bee, too, attached herself to Gigi. It became common-place to see the large female wandering through the forests with the two infants trailing in her wake. Only when Gigi was sexually attrac-tive so that the males gathered around her in large, excited groups, did the orphans separate themselves from their caretaker. Then we often found them on their own, two little babes in the wood.

During a recent visit to Gombe I encountered Gigi feeding on clusters of blossoms, golden yellow in the early-morning sunlight. Above us was the blue sky, and when I looked down the slope I could see the blue water of Lake Tanganyika shimmering through the trees. And feeding contentedly near Gigi were three orphans. For Mel and Dar Bee had been joined by Dharsi, a four-year-old male whose mother had died a few months before.

And so Gigi, although she has never had a baby of her own, was caring for three motherless youngsters, providing for each of them that sense of security that is so desperately important for the grow-ing child – chimpanzee and human child alike. She has truly earned the honorary title we bestowed upon her long ago – Auntie Gigi.

UNDERSTANDING

One day, when I was following David Greybeard through the forest, he stopped to rest beside one of the clear, fast-flowing streams.

I sat near him. It was very peaceful. The sun filtered down through the canopy overhead, speckling the forest floor with golden flecks, dancing on the racing, chattering water. There were secret rustles in the undergrowth as small forest creatures went about their business and birds flitted from branch to branch, searching for food.

I looked at David as he lay, gazing up at the greens and browns of the forest ceiling. He glanced at me, then closed his eyes and slept. As always I was moved by his trust. It has laid a great responsibility on me, for I must never allow that trust to be betrayed. I lay down, there beside him on the forest floor, at peace.

Some time later we roused ourselves. As David sat, looking around, perhaps wondering where to go, I spied a ripe red palm nut lying on the ground nearby. I picked it up and held it towards David, on my palm. He turned his head away. I moved my hand closer. Then David took the nut and, at the same time, closed his fingers around my hand. He glanced into my eyes, let go my hand, then dropped the nut to the ground.

It needed no scientific training to understand the message of reassurance conveyed by the gentle pressure of his fingers over mine – he rejected my gift but not the giving.

His message had no need of words – it was based on a far older form of communication and it bridged the centuries of evolution that divided us.

THE RESEARCH AT GOMBE

Since 1960 we have followed the life histories of more than 100 known chimpanzees. Initially I worked on my own, but subsequently I built up an interdisciplinary team to help with the study.

Chimpanzees are so complex, and differences between individuals so pronounced, that we are still learning new things even after nearly forty years. Since 1975 Tanzanian field staff, recruited from villages surrounding the Gombe National Park, have played a key role in the research. Because they know and care about the chimpanzees and there is no danger of poaching, these chimpanzees whom we have come to know so well can live out their lives in safety.

THE PLIGHT OF CHIMPANZEES ACROSS AFRICA
AND THE WORLD

All across Africa chimpanzees are disappearing fast. This is not only due to the relentless destruction of their forest homes, but also because they are hunted – often for food. Even where they are not eaten, mothers are still shot so that their infants can be stolen, then sold. Some are sold overseas by unscrupulous dealers, for entertainment and for medical research. Some are bought as "pets" by local people, or as attractions in a bar or hotel. For every infant that is bought we estimate that up to ten chimpanzees have died in the forest.

Conditions for chimpanzees in captivity are often grim. In Africa, those bought as pets may spend a few years living as a member of the family, but at adolescence, when they become so strong and potentially dangerous, they are banished to tiny cages or tied up on chains. In African zoos they are often starving (the keepers often cannot afford one meal a day for themselves). Even in the developed world many chimpanzees languish in small, dingy cages, sometimes alone. And in the laboratories they typically live in tiny, bare steel prisons – alone. The training of those used in entertainment is almost always harsh, often cruel. Many are dressed in stupid and inappropriate clothes that give people a completely wrong picture of chimpanzee nature.

It was to try to redress some of these wrongs, as well as to enable us to continue documenting the lives of the Gombe chimpanzees, that the Jane Goodall Institute was established.

THE JANE GOODALL INSTITUTE

Only if we understand can we care
Only if we care will we help
Only if we help shall all be saved

The Jane Goodall Institute was first established in the U.S.A. in 1977. Funds raised by the Institute enable us to continue gathering information about chimpanzees, at Gombe and elsewhere; to conduct conservation efforts; to help improve conditions for captive chimpanzees (and other animals) in zoos, medical research laboratories, and the entertainment trade. Today our work involves research, conservation, welfare, and education in Tanzania, Burundi, Congo, Uganda, Kenya, South Africa, and Ghana, as well as in the U.S.A., Taiwan, and Europe. One of our major efforts is to create sanctuaries for orphan chimpanzees whose mothers have been shot by hunters either for bushmeat or so that their infants can be stolen and sold.

Information about the Institute, how you can join and help us, can be obtained from any of our offices:

JGI (U.S.A.), P.O. Box 599, Ridgefield, Connecticut 06877
JGI (U.K.), 15 Clarendon Park, Lymington, Hampshire S041 8AX
JGI (TZ), P.O. Box 727, Dar es Salaam, Tanzania
JGI (Congo), P.O. Box 1893, Pointe Noire, Congo
JGI (Canada), P.O. Box 477, Victoria Station, Westmount, QC, H3Z 2Y6
JGI (Germany/Austria/Switzerland), Herzogstrasse 60, D–80803 München
JGI (Taiwan ROC), 6F, No. 20 Sec. 2 Hsin–Sheng Sth. Rd, Taipei

ROOTS & SHOOTS

Roots creep underground everywhere and make a firm foundation. Shoots seem very weak, but to reach the light they can break open brick walls. Imagine the brick walls as all the problems humans have inflicted on our planet, from desertification to cruelty and war. Hundreds and thousands of roots and shoots, hundreds and thousands of young people around the world, can break through these walls. Together we can change the world.

Every individual matters
Every individual has a role to play
Every individual makes a difference

The members themselves decide what they can do, individually or as a group, to make the world a better place: by clearing up litter, saving energy, planting trees, caring for animals, and so on; by bringing extra smiles to people's faces, extra wags to the tails of dogs.

The first Roots & Shoots groups were born in Tanzania in February 1991. Today there are hundreds of groups in more than 38 countries; over 600 in North America alone. Through personal correspondence and newsletters members can be in contact with each other around the world. A primary goal, in each country, is to bring together members from different socio-economic and ethnic groups to work on joint projects.

For information on how to start a group, contact any of our offices.

ENTERTAINMENT
TECHNOLOGY

Linda Bruce,
Sam Bruce, and
Jack Bruce

Smart Apple Media

Smart Apple Media
2140 Howard Drive West
North Mankato
Minnesota 56003

First published in 2005 by
MACMILLAN EDUCATION AUSTRALIA PTY LTD
627 Chapel Street, South Yarra, Australia 3141

Visit our Web site at www.macmillan.com.au

Associated companies and representatives throughout the world.

Library of Congress Cataloging-in-Publication Data

Bruce, Linda, 1953-
    Entertainment technology / by Linda Bruce.
      p. cm. – (How does it work?)
    Includes index.
    ISBN-13: 978-1-58340-792-9 (lg. print : hc : alk. paper)
    1. Electronic games—Juvenile literature. 2. Amusements—Technological innovations—Juvenile literature.
    I. Title. II. Series.

GV1469.15.B78 2006
794.8—dc22

                                                                                2005046788

Edited by Anna Fern
Text and cover design by Modern Art Production Group
Illustrations by Andrew Louey
Photo research by Legend Images

Printed in USA

Acknowledgments

The author and publishers are grateful to the following for permission to reproduce copyright material:

Cover photo: Virtual reality game, courtesy of James King-Holmes/W Industries.

AAP, p. 23; Corbis, pp. 28, 29; AP Photo/Richard Drew, p. 16; Rob Cruse Photography, pp. 9, 15, 17; Istockphoto.com, p. 12; Photolibrary.com, pp. 4, 5, 8, 10, 18, 20, 26; Productbank, p. 15; Reuters, pp. 6, 11; © Scott L. Robertson/slrobertson.com , pp. 24, 25; Science Photo Library, /Antonia Reeve, p. 7, /Jerry Mason, p. 14, /James King-Holmes/W Industries, pp. 1, 19, /Kaj R. Svensson, p. 27, /Geoff Tompkinson, p. 30; Siemens, p. 22.

While every care has been taken to trace and acknowledge copyright, the publisher tenders their apologies for any accidental infringement where copyright has proved untraceable. Where the attempt has been unsuccessful, the publisher welcomes information that would redress the situation.

Contents

What is technology? 4

Entertainment technology 5

Computer games 6

Video-game consoles 8

Hand-held games............................... 10

Compact-disc games........................... 12

CD and DVD players........................... 14

Pocket MPEG players 16

Virtual-reality games......................... 18

3-D glasses.................................... 20

Augmented reality 22

Slingshot rides 24

Roller coasters................................ 26

Pendulum rides............................... 28

How well does it work?....................... 30

Glossary...................................... 31

Index... 32

Glossary words

When a word is printed in **bold**, you can look up its meaning in the Glossary on page 31.

What is technology?

Technology helps us to do things. Technology is also about how things work. Since ancient times, people have been interested in how things work, and how they can improve technology to meet their needs. They use their experience, knowledge, and ideas to invent new ways of doing things.

The *How Does It Work?* series features the design and technology of machines that are part of our daily lives. This includes:

- the purpose of the technology and its design
- where it is used
- how it is used
- materials it is made from
- how it works
- future developments

Technology has changed the way we live in many ways. It will keep on bringing change, as people constantly invent new ways of doing things using new materials.

Entertainment technology, such as pinball machines, is enjoyed by people everywhere.

Entertainment technology

Entertainment technology helps us to have fun and enjoy our leisure time.

Over the past 100 years, new technology has revolutionized entertainment. Recordings on records, tapes, and CDs have made music accessible across the world. Photography, film, and video have enabled movies to be made and brought into our living rooms.

Ways of being entertained have changed greatly with the invention of computer technology. Many households have a personal computer, a **console**, or a hand–held computer game. Computer games of endless diversity and complexity are being played on machines that are becoming tiny. Players can pit their wits against the computer, or they can play against people in other parts of the world using the Internet. Amusement parks utilize **simulations** and virtual reality to portray a more realistic experience.

This book takes an inside look at different kinds of entertainment technology. It also previews some amazing new inventions in entertainment technology that you might use in the future.

Virtual-reality games simulate the feeling of being inside the game.

5

Computer games

Computer games are interactive games that can be played on a home computer. Game types include action games, adventure games, role-playing, simulations, strategy and war games, and educational games.

Where used?

Computer games are played on home computers. They are also played on hand-held units, consoles, calculators, cell phones, and in game arcades.

How used?

Computer games can be played by a single person (with the computer as the opponent) or by groups of users who can compete against others anywhere in the world via the Internet. More powerful computers can run games with more complex **graphics** and plots.

Materials

Materials used to make computer games include metal **alloys** and plastic, which are light, durable, and inexpensive. Games incorporate computer intelligence through software, **silicon chips**, or other materials for recording and storing game play.

? Action and adventure games

Arcade games include shooting, fighting, racing, and sport, with typical actions of running, jumping obstacles, stunning monsters or feeding them bananas, and grabbing bonus points or jewels.

Platform games feature scenes, platforms, and increasingly complex mazes for players to advance through, earning points as they go.

In racing games, players choose circuits, from cliff-hanging highways to shooting rapids. Speed, race time, and position on the circuit are displayed on the screen.

Personal computers can run games with complex graphics and plots.

How do computer games work?

A program runs each computer game. When the player commands the game to start, the computer processes the command. It does this with its central processing unit (**CPU**), a series of **circuits** that fits on a fingernail-sized silicon chip.

mouse and keyboard
Commands are input into the game with a keyboard, mouse, joystick, steering wheel, brake, data glove, or other controls.

CPU (central processing unit)
The CPU translates the program commands from binary code into sound and images on screen.

What's next?

In the future, more complex **network** games will be played against large groups of people in different parts of world. When not being played, games systems may be linked with hundreds of other computers to work on complex computing problems, such as deciphering radio signals from space.

? Bits, bytes and megabytes

Computers carry out instructions in "binary code." The code is measured in "bits" which is short for "binary digit." Eight bits equal one byte. A megabyte is one million bytes. A game that is one gigabyte takes up 1,024 megabytes of storage space. A terabyte is approximately one trillion bytes or 1,024 gigabytes.

Video-game consoles

A video-game console is used to run computer games. A television is used as a display screen.

Where used?

Consoles are plugged into televisions. Over 29 million people worldwide play games on consoles. Consoles are less expensive than personal computers.

How used?

Console games can be played by a single person or by a group, each holding a controller. To play the game, players press buttons or joysticks on the game pad. The command travels along the wire to the console. The console sends a signal to the television monitor and action appears on the television screen, together with sound.

Materials

Materials selected to make consoles include plastic casings and wire leads that do not break easily when bumped. Silicon-chip **microprocessors** run the game programs.

Unlike games on a personal computer, console games do not need to be installed and can be played immediately by inserting a game cartridge or disc.

How video-game consoles work

Video games are stored on CD, **CD-ROM** cartridges, or **DVD**. The game is pushed into a slot in the console. The console contains a DVD drive, a computer (often with a built-in **hard drive**), a graphics processor, audio processor, and **memory card**. The computer decodes the software and displays graphics on the television screen.

Some consoles can play DVD movies and games, and **download** games from the Internet. Others store saved games, some of which can be transferred to and played on cell phones, calculators, and personal computers.

The sound and picture signals go from here to the television.

control pad
Video games are played with buttons or joysticks on the control pad.

storage
Game software is stored on a compact disc or cartridge.

What's next?

In the future, video-game consoles will be powerful enough to incorporate virtual-reality technology, such as **3-D** glasses. Video-game consoles may network with other consoles across the world. Like computers, game consoles are constantly improving.

Hand-held games

Hand-held games are small, portable devices that contain built-in computer games.

Where used?

Hand-held game units are small enough to be carried in pockets. They can be used anywhere—at home, at school, and while travelling.

How used?

The unit is held in one hand and the player pushes buttons to control the game action. Movements often include jumping, running, blasting obstacles, leaping onto vines and across chasms, and grabbing bonus jewels and lollypops.

Materials

The game case and screen are made of plastic, which looks good and is sturdy. They come in many fashionable colors and some people like to collect them as well as play them. Inside, the **circuitry** includes silicon chips and metal wiring.

Battery-operated hand-held games can be played anywhere.

How hand-held games work

Hand-held games have built-in games and a tiny computer powered by batteries. The games often require hand–eye coordination to move bats under balls or fit moving blocks into holes. They also feature action figures, which players command to jump, run, throw, and shoot.

liquid crystal display
The screen may display **32,000 shades of color.**

controls
The game is played by pressing the directional pad and left and right shoulder buttons.

speaker

batteries
Inside the game, two AA disposable or rechargeable batteries allow up to 20 hours of playing time.

What's next?

In the future, games with wireless radio connections will enable two players, each with a hand-held game, to compete against each other.

Compact-disc games

Compact-disc games feature complex images and sound stored on a CD-ROM or DVD.

Where used?

Compact-disc games are played on personal computers, often at home.

How used?

The disc is placed in the disc drive, the game launches, and the player follows on-screen game instructions to play the game. The game can be viewed on a computer and copied from disc to computer, but the information on the disc itself cannot be changed. A DVD can hold at least seven times more information than a CD-ROM. DVDs hold games, encyclopedias, or movies that would otherwise require multiple CDs with constant disc changing during playing.

Materials

Discs are made from polycarbonate plastic with a thin layer of **aluminum**.

? Single and double-sided DVDs

A DVD may be recorded on one or two sides, and have one or two layers per side. Double-layered sides look gold, while single-layered sides look silver. A single-sided, single-layered disc stores 4.7 gigabytes of information. A double-sided, double-layered disc stores 18.8 gigabytes.

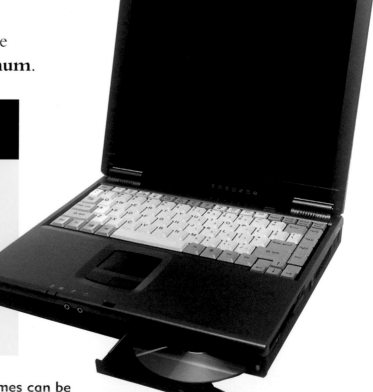

Compact-disc games can be played on laptops and personal computers.

How do compact disc games work?

The information on a compact disc is stored as a track of tiny bumps which spiral out from the center of the disc. When the disc is placed in the disc drive, it spins at between 200 and 500 revolutions per minute. A **laser** light inside the player follows the spiral track. The reflective surface of the CD reflects the laser light off the bumps so that the player can read the disc and convert the digital information into sound and video.

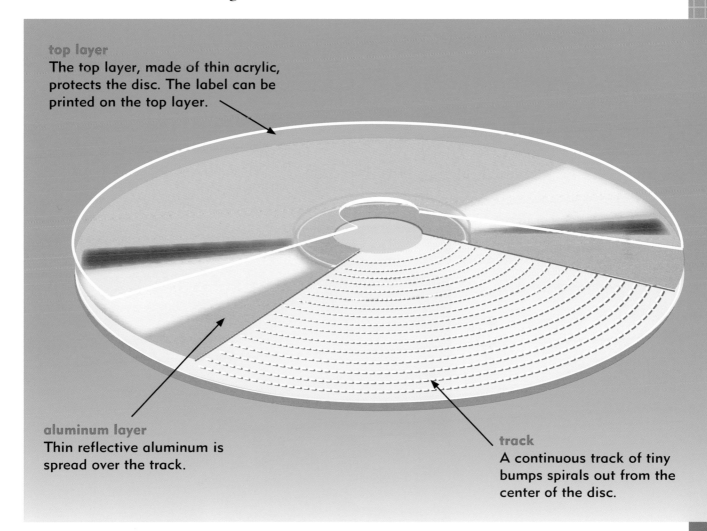

top layer
The top layer, made of thin acrylic, protects the disc. The label can be printed on the top layer.

aluminum layer
Thin reflective aluminum is spread over the track.

track
A continuous track of tiny bumps spirals out from the center of the disc.

What's next?

In the future, smaller discs and memory cards will store much more information.

CD and DVD players

A CD or DVD player uses a laser to read a compact disc and translate this information into graphics and sound. CD and DVD players can play music, videos, computer games, computer programs, and most other digitally encoded information.

Where used?

Some CD and DVD players can be used as a separate unit, or they can be connected to a television or sound system. They are often built into personal computers and game consoles.

How used?

When the disc is placed in the player, the drive reads the disc. The CD or DVD player can be controlled by pushing controls on the player, or by giving commands through a remote control, keyboard, mouse, joystick, or other input device.

Materials

Materials selected include sturdy metal wiring, a protective plastic case, and a laser light to read tiny tracks on the disc.

CD and DVD players can read and play back digital entertainment.

How CD and DVD players work

CD and DVD players read information stored as bumps on the disc and translate them into images and sound. Attached to the CD or DVD player, a screen displays graphics and speakers play the sound.

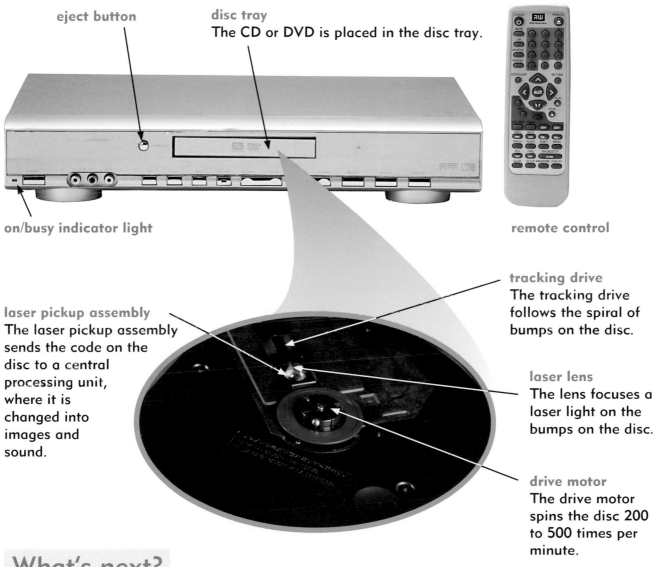

eject button

disc tray
The CD or DVD is placed in the disc tray.

on/busy indicator light

remote control

tracking drive
The tracking drive follows the spiral of bumps on the disc.

laser pickup assembly
The laser pickup assembly sends the code on the disc to a central processing unit, where it is changed into images and sound.

laser lens
The lens focuses a laser light on the bumps on the disc.

drive motor
The drive motor spins the disc 200 to 500 times per minute.

What's next?

In the future, faster Internet connections may enable games, music, or movies to be accessed over the Internet, instead of being stored on discs and played by individual disc drives. Players will pay to access the game, run the movie, or download the music. Discs will not be needed.

Pocket MPEG players

A pocket MPEG player can be used to watch movies, listen to music, or play games.

Where used?

MPEG players can be used anywhere. They are small enough to be carried in a pocket, or to be clipped to a belt or armband.

How used?

The user presses buttons on the case to input commands, such as selecting a program, video, or game. MPEG entertainment can be bought on CD or DVD, or downloaded from the Internet. The MPEG player can be connected by a lead to a personal computer, so that entertainment can be transferred from the computer to the player.

Materials

The MPEG player case is made of strong plastic. Inside, the circuitry includes a silicon chip for reading and playing the program, and wires made from metal alloys. MPEG players are made with a minimum of moving parts so that play is unaffected by movement.

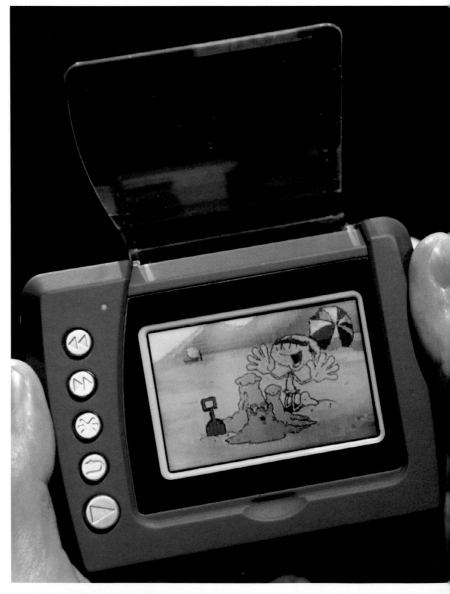

Pocket MPEG players can play games, movies, TV, and songs.

How do MPEG players work?

MPEG players have a mini-computer for storing and playing digital MPEG entertainment. Inside the player, a microprocessor reads MPEG encoded entertainment, and plays it over a display. The display can be a small built-in screen, or sometimes the MPEG player can be connected to an external screen.

personal computer
Music can be downloaded from the Internet via a personal computer. When the data has been downloaded, a cable is plugged from the computer to the MPEG player and the music can be copied across to the MPEG player.

CPU
Inside, the CPU (central processing unit) reads the digital information stored on the MPEG player and changes it into sound and pictures.

cable
The cable enables MPEG files to be transferred from the computer to the MPEG player.

What's next?

In the future, MPEG players will have sharper pictures and will be cheaper. More players will link with other people's MPEG players using a wireless connection.

Virtual-reality games

A virtual-reality game uses a computer to create the experience of being inside the game itself.

Where used?

Virtual-reality (VR) games are played at home with a personal computer, and in video arcades and theme parks.

How used?

Players wear VR equipment designed to create experiences, such as sound, touch, and movement. Equipment may include display screens, 3-D masks, data gloves, and devices, such as waist tethers, to tell the computer where the player is within the game. Movement detectors built into head displays enable the computer to create views that players would see as they turn their head and walk within the game. For example, players can view birds swooping, or a monster following them.

Materials

Materials selected to make VR equipment include metal, plastic, and silicon chips.

Virtual-reality headsets provide views for each direction in which a player looks.

How do virtual-reality games work?

Virtual reality enables players to move around in a computer-generated 3-D environment. Realistic, 3-D holographic images are created by a video being projected onto a special surface. Players may compete against life-size **holograms** of people, animals, and monsters, or see virtual racing cars whiz past.

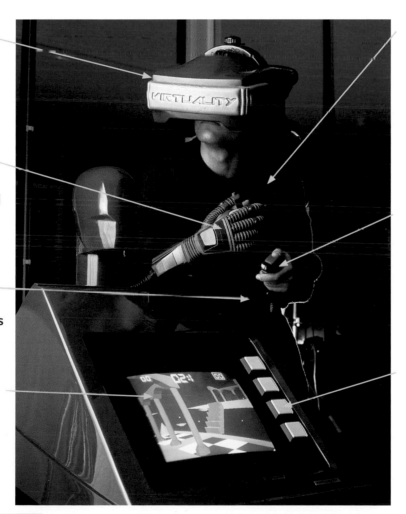

headset
The headset provides a view of the direction in which the player looks.

data glove
The data glove enables the player to move their hand inside the game.

waist sensor
The waist sensor detects the player's position.

playing platform
The playing platform defines where the action takes place.

vest
The vest can detect and record when a player has been hit by an **infrared light** beam from another player's laser gun.

equipment
Players may use laser guns, steering wheels, or other virtual-reality equipment.

computer software system

What's next?

In the future, VR technology for home use will include headsets with stereo sound and vision, games that respond to voice commands, and holograms to create scenes around players. VR goggles will display 3-D images which change in response to the user's actions and positions.

3-D glasses

Watching 3-D movies requires the viewer to wear 3-D glasses. The glasses provide viewers with a realistic experience of visual depth.

Where used?

People use 3-D glasses to watch 3-D movies at home and in movie theaters. 3-D movies are made up of two images projected onto a screen. 3-D glasses allow only one image to enter each eye, and you see this as depth.

How used?

Watching a 3-D movie can make the action seem so realistic that, for example, viewers feel that they are walking on the edge of a cliff, or that animals come so close that they can be touched. Without 3-D glasses, a 3-D movie looks blurred.

Materials

One type of 3-D glasses is made with sturdy plastic frames and lenses. Other 3-D glasses are made from paper and colored cellophane, which is inexpensive, flexible, and light to wear.

3-D movies can seem so realistic that audiences feel they are part of the action on the screen.

How do 3-D glasses work?

We see depth around us because each of our two eyes sees slightly different images. 3-D glasses create the impression of depth by feeding a different image into each eye.

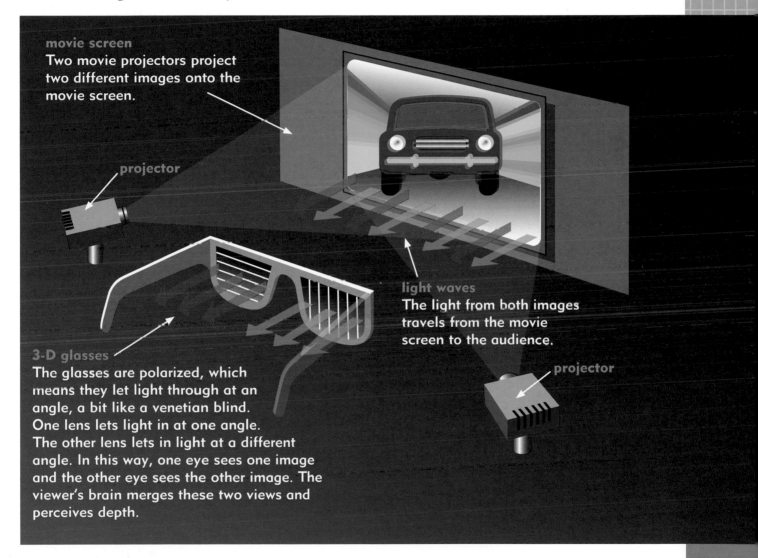

movie screen
Two movie projectors project two different images onto the movie screen.

projector

3-D glasses
The glasses are polarized, which means they let light through at an angle, a bit like a venetian blind. One lens lets light in at one angle. The other lens lets in light at a different angle. In this way, one eye sees one image and the other eye sees the other image. The viewer's brain merges these two views and perceives depth.

light waves
The light from both images travels from the movie screen to the audience.

projector

What's next?

In the future, movies may use holograms and virtual-reality technology to enable viewers to feel like they are walking around inside the action. Instead of being projected onto a screen in a large theater, movies will be screened into the viewers' goggles.

Augmented reality

Augmented-reality systems add or join graphics, sounds, and even the sense of touch and smell to the natural world. In augmented reality, computer graphics are overlaid onto a live video picture, or projected onto a transparent screen, such as in glasses. In this way extra information is added to what is being experienced.

Where used?

Augmented reality is in its early stages of development. It has been used in computer games, in some hi-tech museums as a tourist attraction, and in the military to help troops find their way around and to identify buildings and objects.

How used?

Augmented-reality glasses overlay information and sound on a normal view. They may be linked to **satellite** global positioning systems.

Materials

Augmented-reality devices may involve special glasses or headsets that are sensitive to place, using small computing and display devices. Materials are selected to be easy to maintain, safe, and comfortable to use.

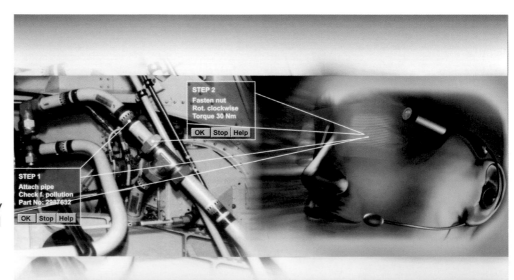

Augmented-reality adds graphics and sounds to the real world.

How augmented reality works

Augmented-reality graphics are coordinated so they change with the wearer's head movements. Augmented-reality systems recognize objects the wearer is looking at, and display information about that view in the wearer's goggles. For example, in an augmented-reality game, you may find yourself racing a virtual car against a real televized race on television.

tracking system
A personal locator uses a satellite signal to locate a person in their surroundings in order to provide correct information.

head-mounted display
A see-through overlay displays text and graphics as well as the wearer's natural surroundings. Sound is also added. Other devices may be used to simulate touch or even smell.

Small batteries in the player's backpack provide power. A built-in mobile computer processes the data.

What's next?

In the future, augmented reality technology may focus on a person's inner state as well as their surroundings. For example, if a person is stressed, calming images and instructions may be superimposed to help them cope better.

23

Slingshot rides

The slingshot ride simulates a rocket launch by propelling a capsule attached to steel cables straight up into the air.

Where used?

This ride is used in amusement parks. Every ride has safety rules, and there are often restrictions on riders' age, height and weight, and warnings for people who suffer from medical conditions, such as weak hearts or neck injuries.

How used?

Riders sit in a metal capsule. Metal bars hold them into their seats. The capsule tilts so riders are lying on their backs. A loudspeaker counts down "3, 2, 1." Then the **magnet** releases and the capsule shoots over 330 feet (100 m) high and more than 130 feet (40 m) past the top of the support towers.

Materials

The springs, ropes, and pulleys of the ride are made from strong steel.

The slingshot ride shoots riders into the air.

How slingshot rides work

The slingshot capsule sits on a specially designed, powerful spring held down by a huge magnet. When the magnet is turned off, the capsule launches straight up at speeds of more than 100 miles (160 km) per hour. A computer senses spring tension and ensures that every rider, whether light or heavy, receives an equal amount of thrust. When the capsule returns, the spring machine hurls it back up again, flipping the capsule over and over.

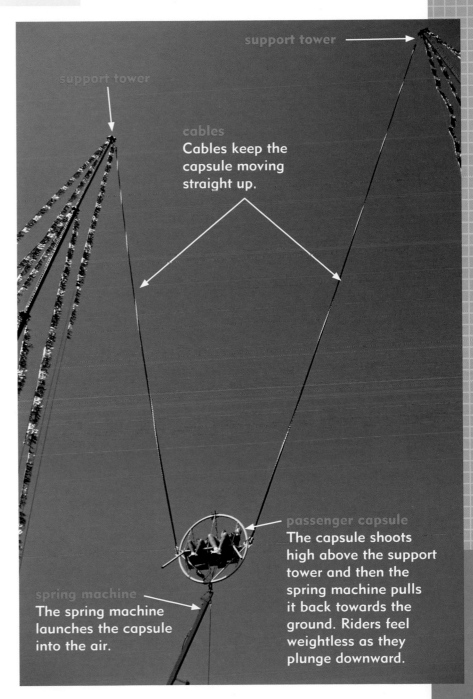

support tower

support tower

cables
Cables keep the capsule moving straight up.

passenger capsule
The capsule shoots high above the support tower and then the spring machine pulls it back towards the ground. Riders feel weightless as they plunge downward.

spring machine
The spring machine launches the capsule into the air.

What's next?

In the future, amusement parks may have rocket sleds that hit **hypersonic** speeds of Mach 8.5, or 6,429 miles (10,352 km) per hour.

Roller coasters

A roller-coaster ride provides excitement, unexpected twists, turns and dips, and a sense of danger while being completely safe for riders.

Where used?

Roller coasters are found in amusement parks. Invented in the United States, they are popular all over the world.

How used?

Riders sit in cars, with a bar over their lap to hold them so they cannot fall out.

The coaster is towed to the top of a steep track. Then it descends, racing around sharp bends creating a feeling of danger for the riders. Finally, it stops back at the station.

Materials

Roller coasters are mainly made from metals that are strong, durable, easy to maintain, and minimally affected by changes of condition. Tracks are made from long steel tubes supported by strong, light, slightly larger steel tubes or beams. The coaster wheels are made from strong man-made substances, such as polyurethane or nylon.

Roller coasters give riders the exciting feeling that they are in danger.

How roller coasters work

Roller coasters are dragged to the top of a track by a motor. Once at the top of the track, the roller coaster uses **gravity** to speed down the track, going faster and faster. As the ride progresses, the track continually loses height, which causes the roller coaster to speed up, and gains height, which makes it slow down.

Preventing collisions

Electromagnet sensors in the roller coaster track prevent train collision by detecting metal "flags" on the trains. Flags on the front and rear of the train tell the computer the train has entered and left a particular section of the track.

clamps
When the roller coaster is upside down, it is rigidly attached to the track.

brakes
Brakes built into the track clamp closed on metal fins running under the train to slow the roller coaster.

wheels
Wheels on top of the track keep the train running smoothly. Wheels under the track and along the sides anchor the car to the track during dips and turns.

track

What's next?

In the future, higher, faster roller coasters may be combined with even scarier video backdrops, such as going inside a volcano or over cliffs.

Pendulum rides

A pendulum ride is like a swing. It gradually swings higher and higher, and sometimes completes a circle.

Where used?

Pendulum rides are found in amusement parks all over the world.

How used?

Riders step from the station platform into a boat. Bars around their arms and body prevent them from falling out. The boat swings in an increasing arc until it completes a full circle. It then rocks back to a stop at the completion of the ride. When the ride completes a 360-degree circle, the boat turns upside down and riders experience a feeling of complete weightlessness.

Materials

The boat swing may be made from molded metal and heavy-duty synthetic materials. Cables are made from strong steel. These materials require little maintenance and can withstand heat, cold, rain, and wind.

Pendulum rides swing higher and higher until they complete a full circle.

How pendulum rides work

Pendulum rides swing a boat in an arc between two main towers. At the bottom of the arc, pendulum riders experience a feeling of high gravity forces as they are pressed into their seats. At the top of the arc, riders feel weightless, as the seat is not pressing on them and they are free-falling.

? Why do you feel sick?

The fast rocking, swinging, and changes of angle and speed on amusement-park rides often produce motion sickness. This is caused by a difference between what you see and the parts in your ear that sense motion. Receiving too much information for your body to process can also make you feel sick.

capsule
The boat swings along the track in an increasing arc, pausing at the top of each arc before it is pulled back down by gravity. When high enough, the boat sometimes completes a full circle.

safety bar
Riders are held in their seats by a metal bar.

entry platform
Riders step into the boat here.

What's next?

In the future, pendulum rides may swing between 50-story-high towers. Virtual reality may give riders the exact experience of being on a pendulum ride without leaving the ground.

How well does it work?

In this book you have read about and looked at the designs of many different technologies. As well as understanding how technology works, we also need to think about how well it works in relation to other needs, such as aesthetic, environmental, and social needs. We can judge how well the idea, product, or process works by considering questions, such as:

Manufacture	• Is the manufacture of the technology efficient in its use of energy and resources?
Usability	• Does the technology do the job it is designed to do? • Is it safe to use? • Is it easy to use?
Social impact	• Does it have any negative effects on people?
Environmental impact	• Does using the technology have any environmental effects? • Does it create noise, cause pollution, or create any waste products?
Aesthetics	• Does the design fit into its surroundings and look attractive?

Thinking about these sorts of questions can help people to invent improved ways of doing things.

Virtual reality and simulated experiences bring a new level of thrills to computer-game technology.

Glossary

alloys mixtures of metals

aluminum a strong, light metal which resists rust, and conducts electricity and heat well

CD-ROM (compact disc read only memory) a disc that can store up to 650 megabytes of data

circuits paths between two or more points along which an electrical current or signal can be carried

circuitry a system of electrical circuits

console a device used for direct communication with a computer system

CPU (Central Processing Unit) the silicon chip "brain" of the computer—the more powerful the chip, the faster programs run

download copy file from a central Internet server

DVD (digital versatile disc) physically similar to a CD, a DVD can store up to 17 gigabytes of data

electromagnet a magnet that needs electricity to activate it

graphics anything displayed on a computer screen that is not text

gravity a force that pulls objects back to the surface of Earth

hard drive the main device in a computer that is used to permanently store and retrieve information

holograms flat images that appear to be three-dimensional

hypersonic speeds of five times the speed of sound (Mach 5) or higher

infrared light a wavelength of electromagnetic radiation that is similar to the wavelength of red light, but which is invisible to the human eye

laser a highly focused beam of light which can produce immense heat and power when focused at close range

magnet metal that can pull iron or steel objects toward it and hold or move them

memory card a credit-card-sized card that can store digital data

microprocessor the central processing unit (CPU) or silicon-chip "brain" of a computer

network a group of connected computers that can communicate with one another

satellite a machine placed in orbit around Earth to perform a job, such as relaying communications signals

silicon chip a wafer-thin slice of silicon, smaller than a fingernail, which contains thousands of microscopic electronic circuits

simulations computer games that imitate a real-world experience.

3-D (three dimensional) having, or appearing to have, length, width, and depth

uploaded to copy a file from a personal computer to an Internet server

Index

A aesthetics 30
amusement parks 5, 18, 24–25,
   26–27, 28–29
augmented reality 22–23

C CD players 13, 14–15
CD-ROMs 9, 12–13, 14–15, 16
cell phones 6, 9
central processing unit (CPU) 7, 17
computer games 5, 6–7, 8–9, 10–11,
   12–13, 16

D design 4, 30
DVD players 14–15
DVDs 9, 12, 14–15, 16

E entertainment 5
environmental effects 30

G global positioning systems 22

H hand-held games 6, 10–11
holograms 19, 21

I Internet 5, 9, 15, 16, 17
inventions 4, 30

L laser light 13, 15
liquid crystal displays 11

M manufacture 30
motion sickness 29
movies 5, 12, 16, 20–21
MPEG 16–17
MPEG players 16–17
music 5, 16–17

P pendulum rides 28–29
personal computers 5, 6–7, 9, 12, 14,
   16, 17, 18
portable entertainment 10–11,
   16–17, 22–23

R roller coasters 26–27

S safety 30
silicon chips 6, 8, 10, 16, 18
slingshot rides 24–25
software 6–7, 9, 12–13, 19

T technology (definition) 4
television 8
three-dimensional glasses 9, 18, 19,
   20–21

V video-game consoles 6, 8–9, 14
virtual reality 5, 18–19, 21